The Ultimate
Lemur
Book for Kids

Jenny Kellett

BELLANOVA

MELBOURNE · SOFIA · BERLIN

Copyright © 2026 by Jenny Kellett

The Ultimate Lemur Book
www.bellanovabooks.com

Verify this book's Human-Approved Certification at
www.authorwing.com/verify

ISBN: 978-619-264-072-9
Imprint: Bellanova Books

All rights reserved. No part of this book may be reproduced in any form by any electronic or mechanical means including photocopying, recording, or information storage and retrieval without permission in writing from the author.

CONTENTS

Introduction 4
Lemur Facts - The Basics 6
Madagascar 16
Lemur Species 20
    Family: Cheirogaleidae 22
    Family: Lemuridae 26
        Ring-tailed Lemurs 30
    Family: Lepilemuridae 36
    Family: Indriidae 40
    Family: Daubentoniidae 44
From Birth to Adulthood 48
Their Daily Lives 58
Their Future 68
More Facts 76
Lemur Quiz 84
    Answers 89
Word search 90
Sources 92

INTRODUCTION

There are few creatures more adorable than lemurs. Their fluffy tails and bright, wide eyes are hard not to love. But how much do you really know about them? In this book, we take a deeper look at the lemur and you'll be amazed at what you'll learn.

My first encounter with lemurs was at Melbourne Zoo in Australia. There is a special area just for lemurs that you can walk around, and they are very friendly! On the right is one of the resident ring-tailed lemurs.

So are you ready to learn more? *Let's go!*

LEMURS:
THE BASICS

WHAT ARE LEMURS AND WHERE DO THEY LIVE?

Lemurs are **mammals**. They are also **primates**, which is a group of mammals that includes gorillas, monkeys, orangutans, and us: humans.

• • •

There are eight families of lemurs (three of which are now extinct) and around 100 different species! The number of species is constantly changing as new ones are discovered.

A black and white ruffed lemur.

A sifaka lemur.

There are more species of lemurs than any other species of primate. This is thanks to the varied climate of their homeland.

• • •

Lemurs only live in the wild in **Madagascar**, which is an island off the east coast of Africa.

• • •

Before humans arrived in Madagascar around 2,000 years ago, there were species of lemurs the size of gorillas! Now, most species are quite small.

The size and weight of lemurs vary a lot between the different species — from the 1.1 oz (33 g) **mouse lemur** to the 10 lb (9 kg) **indri lemur**.

• • •

Lemurs can live up to 30 years old in captivity, and about half that in the wild.

• • •

Lemurs don't have great vision, and most can only see in partial or no color. They rely heavily on their sense of smell.

A ring-tailed lemur sitting in a tree   >

Ring-tailed lemurs.

A male greater bamboo lemur.
Source: Chris Sharp, sharpphotography.co.uk

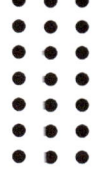

Lemurs have scent glands in different parts of their bodies that help them to leave markers and communicate with other lemurs.

Ruffed lemurs have a scent gland in the back of their necks, whereas the **greater bamboo lemur** has one at the top of its arm.

• • •

As you know, lemurs call the island of Madagascar home. So let's take a closer look at this beautiful place.

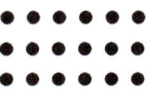

THE ULTIMATE LEMUR BOOK

MADAGASCAR
A lush, wild, and magical island

Madagascar is located 250 miles off the east coast of Africa. It is the fourth largest island in the world and is home to a huge amount of wildlife (flora and fauna) that can't be found anywhere else in the world. Sadly, because the wildlife there is so rare, it is also at risk of extinction.

The human population of Madagascar is more than that of Australia or Greece; there are around 27 million people living there. People from Madagascar are called **Malagasy**.

Two-thirds of the world's chameleon species live in Madagascar.

Madagascar was only discovered in 500AD, which is relatively young compared to other countries. It is because of this that so many interesting animals and plants managed to evolve and thrive on Madagascar.

Although the country is rich in biodiversity, it remains one of the poorest countries in the world.

However, an increase in tourists (many of whom come to see animals such as lemurs) is providing more jobs to the locals.

So how did lemurs get to Madagascar? Originally, lemurs lived on mainland Africa, but it's believed they rafted across the Indian Ocean to Madagascar on large pieces of vegetation before evolving into the species we know today. Before humans arrived, lemurs had no predators on the island.

LEMUR SPECIES

As you're about to find out, lemurs come in all different shapes and sizes! Within the five families of lemur there are over 100 subspecies—each with their own unique traits.

So let's dive in and see what the differences are.

A ring-tailed lemur.

Family: Cheirogaleidae

Species include: *mouse and dwarf lemurs.*

There are 34 living species of lemurs in the Cheirogaleidae family. These include the tiny **mouse lemurs** and **dwarf lemurs**. **Madame Berthe's mouse lemur** is the smallest lemur species and smallest primate in the world.

Other species in the family include the **fat-tailed dwarf lemur, furry-eared dwarf lemur**, and the **Masoala fork-marked lemur**.

Cheirogaleids have long, soft fur, which is usually bright on their bellies, and a greyish-brown to reddish color on the main part of their bodies.

Brown mouse lemur.
Source: Heinonlein on Wikipedia

Madame Berthe's mouse lemur—the smallest species of lemur. *Source: FC Casuario*

They are always very tiny, growing to a maximum size of 5-11" (13-28 cm). Often their tails are one and a half times as long as their bodies!

Like many other lemurs, Cheirogaleids are nocturnal and live almost entirely in the trees, where they like to hide out in the hollows. Using their long tails, they balance themselves as they jump from tree to tree. They spend most of their lives alone, but can occasionally be found in pairs.

Cheirogaleids aren't fussy eaters and they will eat anything from leaves and fruits to insects and spiders.

Family: Lemuridae

Species include: *Ring-tailed, bamboo and ruffed lemurs*

The Lemuridae family of lemurs contains many of the species you are probably familiar with, such as the ring-tailed lemur, black-and-white ruffed lemur, and common brown lemur.

There are 21 species within this family, which can be divided into five sub-groups:
- Genus *Lemur*
- Genus *Eulemur* (true lemurs),
- Genus *Varecia* (ruffed lemurs),
- Genus *Hapalemur* (bamboo lemurs),
- Genus *Pachylemur* (now extinct, but contained giant lemurs), and
- Genus *Prolemur.*

A female common brown lemur with her juvenile. *Source: Sharpphotography.co.uk*

Unlike mouse and dwarf lemurs, lemurids are very sociable and often live in groups of around 30 other lemurs.

Lemurids are **herbivores**, meaning they only eat plants. They eat a lot of fruit, and sometimes even nectar from flowers.

They are of an average size, and range between 12.6-22" (32-56 cm) in length.

Their tails are long and bushy and their fur comes in many different colors, including red, black and white and grey.

< **Red ruffed lemur.** *Source: Sharpphotography.co.uk*

RING-TAILED LEMUR

Scientific name: *Lemur catta*

Ring-tailed lemurs are probably the most famous species of lemur so let's look at them in a bit more detail. If you go to a zoo, you will probably see a ring-tailed lemur. They are easily recognizable thanks to their bushy, stripy black and white tails. Ring-tailed lemurs live in the southwest corner of Madagascar.

Not only are they adorable, but they have many characteristics that are different from other lemurs. Ring-tailed lemurs spend almost a third of their time on the ground, so their diet is different from many other lemurs.

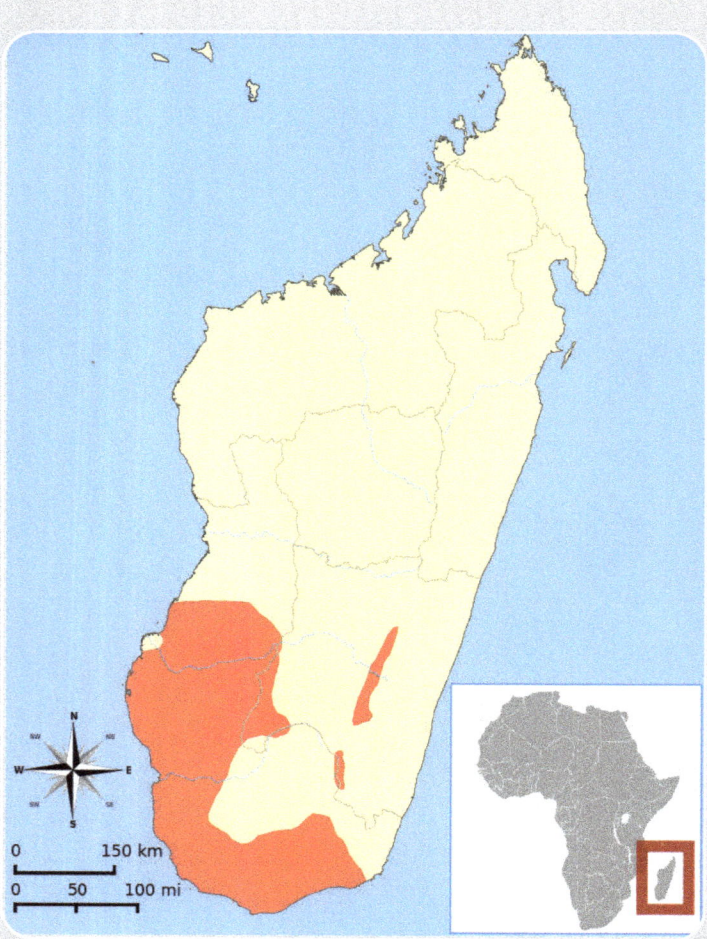

The area where ring-tailed lemurs live. *Source: IUCN Red List of Threatened Species*

Their favorite food is **tamarind leaves**, which are found closer to the forest floor.

When they are on the ground, they hold their tails up high as they walk around so that other members of the group can see them.

Ring-tailed lemurs are the most vocal lemur species. They will talk to each other with a range of sounds and calls.

They are also very sociable and can often be found huddling together, particularly when it's cold.

Despite having relatively small brains, ring-tailed lemurs are very smart and can understand simple arithmetic and even pick tools for basic tasks!

Ring-tailed lemurs are **diurnal**, meaning they are active during the day and sleep at night.

Although you can find them all around the world in zoos, ring-tailed lemurs are listed as **endangered**. Their habitats are being destroyed and they are often illegally hunted. There are now more ring-tailed lemurs living in zoos than there are in the wild.

FAMILY: LEPILEMURIDAE

Species include: Holland's sportive lemur, James' sportive lemur and Seal's sportive lemur

This family is made up of 26 different species of sportive lemurs, sadly, nine of which are critically endangered.

Sportive lemurs are medium-size and have grey-brown to reddish fur on top and white-yellowish fur on their bellies. They have large ears and small round heads and have shiny eyes thanks to their tapetum lucidum reflective layer.

Ankarana sportive lemur. >
Credit: Sharp Photography

Small-toothed sportive lemur.
Source: Edward E. Louis Jr.

Sportive lemurs are nocturnal and live only in trees. They have strong hind legs that help them jump long distances between trees.

When they are occasionally on the ground they hop around like kangaroos!

Generally, sportive lemurs prefer to live alone and are quite territorial if another lemur of the same sex tries to approach them.

Sportive lemur subspecies' include the **grey-backed sportive lemur, weasel sportive lemur, red-tailed sportive lemur**, and **small-toothed sportive lemur**.

FAMILY: INDRIIDAE

Species include: eastern woolly lemur, indri, silky sifaka and Coquerel's sifaka

The Indriidae family of lemurs contains 19 species including the **indri**, the largest living species of lemur, as well as **woolly lemurs** and **sifakas**.

They are an interesting family because they vary so much in size and characteristics. For example, the **avahi lemurs** are only 12" (30 cm) in length compared to the huge **indri** at 25-28" (64-72 cm). Also, the indri only has a stub for a tail, while **avahi and sifaka lemurs** have tails as long as their bodies.

Indri lemur in a tree.

There are a couple of similarities, though. Their fur is long and is usually a white, red or grey color, and they all have bald, black faces.

All indriids are herbivores, meaning they only eat plants. Unlike other species of lemurs, indriids have only four front teeth, instead of six.

Indriids live in trees but when they do come down to the ground, they hop forward on two legs with their arms in the air. They are relatively social and live in groups of around 15 others. Indriids also love to sun themselves, so are often seen lying around stretched out in the trees!

< **Dancing sifaka lemur.**

FAMILY: DAUBENTONIIDAE

Species: Aye-Aye

The Daubentoniidae family of lemurs is the smallest one, as it contains only one living species — the **aye-aye**, which lives mostly on the east coast of Madagascar.

The aye-aye lemur has long fingers, including a special thin middle finger. They have rodent-like teeth that continually grow and are the world's largest nocturnal primates. They can reach lengths of 3 ft (90 cm) and their tails are longer than their bodies.

Aye-ayes spend most of their time alone but occasionally work in teams to forage for food.

A wild Aye-Aye. Notice his long fingers.
Source: Nomis Simon

Aye-ayes have a very interesting way of searching for food. They use their thin middle finger to tap on trees to find insects, then drill small holes in the wood with their teeth before using their long fourth finger to pull out their meal. This way of searching for food is called **percussive foraging**, and only one other animal is known to use this method — the striped possum.

Female aye-ayes have only two nipples, which are located near the groin region.

Young aye-ayes are usually silver on their fronts with a stripe of fur down their backs, but once they grow up they are covered in thick fur of multiple colors.

An Aye-Aye at night. *Source: Frank Vassen*

Aye-aye's live high up in the trees and are **omnivores**, meaning they eat both plants and meat. They can spend around 80% of each night foraging for food.

Interestingly, their highly evolved ears mean that they can use echolocation to find food — the only mammal to do so!

FROM BIRTH TO ADULTHOOD

LET'S LEARN MORE ABOUT THE EARLY LIFE OF LEMURS.

Baby lemurs are called **pups**.

...

For most lemurs, there are only three weeks of the year where they mate. This is because of the constantly changing climate in Madagascar. They try to make sure that there will be plenty of food available for when the young lemurs arrive.

A diademed sifaka lemur pup.

The **gestation period** (how long a female is pregnant) varies quite a lot between the species. While mouse lemurs are pregnant for only 60 days, sportive lemurs need between 120-150 days.

...

The small nocturnal lemurs, such as mouse lemurs, give birth to multiple young, whereas the larger lemurs usually only have one. However, the ruffed lemurs are the only large lemurs to give birth to 2-3 young each time, and sometimes up to six!

<   A young Coquerel's sifaka taking a ride with its mother.

When looking for the right mate, it comes down to smell. Male lemurs will spray their tails with urine and wave them around. The lemur with the smelliest tail will usually win the female!

...

When **ruffed lemur** pups are born they aren't fully developed, so their mothers build nests for them to stay in.

...

A newborn **ring-tailed lemur** pup weighs around 3 oz (100 g).

A ring-tailed lemur feeding her pup.

A family of ring-tailed lemurs.

All species of lemurs, except the sportive lemur and the aye-aye, have been seen to co-parent or share parenting responsibilities with other lemurs. Sometimes, males will even take care of the pups.

Once they are born, many lemur species' pups will cling onto their mother's stomachs for the first few weeks of their lives. After that, they will ride on her back until they are 3-4 months old.

...

Sometimes lemur mothers will stash their young inside the hollow of trees while they go foraging.

...

Bamboo lemurs carry their pups around in their mouths by the scruff of their neck for the first few weeks, until they are strong enough to cling onto their bellies.

Once pups are between 3-6 months old (depending on the species), they are fully weaned and can start foraging for their own food.

However, they can start eating solid food when they are around two months old.

...

Lemurs have a long lifespan, but sadly a large number of pups die.

A ring-tailed lemur pup enjoying a healthy snack. >

LEMURS' DAILY LIVES

The daily life and behavior of lemurs really vary depending on the species. Some species are nocturnal, others diurnal and all sorts of variations in between! They also have different diets and breeding patterns.

In general, smaller species of lemurs are omnivores — meaning they eat plants and insects, while the larger species are herbivores. However, a hungry lemur will usually eat anything it can find.

A red ruffed lemur.

A ring-tailed lemur sitting on the ground.

Around 55% of known plant species in Madagascar are eaten by lemurs.

• • •

Although lemurs aren't fussy, they rarely eat mangroves and ferns as they don't have a great taste.

• • •

The **greater bamboo lemur**, as the name suggests, eats almost entirely bamboo. Bamboo contains large amounts of the poison cyanide, which would be lethal to most mammals, but obviously not to them!

Social species of lemurs will groom each other to solidify their relationships.

They do this by licking the fur and then scraping out any bugs or dirt with their toothcombs.

• • •

Most small lemurs are nocturnal, while larger lemurs are diurnal.

• • •

Mouse and **dwarf lemurs** are the only primates that hibernate. During this time their heart and metabolic rate slow down.

A Coquerel's sifaka.

Bamboo lemurs.

Mouse lemurs may hibernate for a few days at a time, while dwarf lemurs can hibernate for up to eight months of the year!

...

Instead of hibernating when food is scarce, other lemurs will huddle together in groups or take shelter in warm tree hollows.

...

Lemurs have interesting ways of getting around when they are on the ground. For example, sifakas will leap on their hind legs sidewards in what looks like a dance, while other lemurs will walk on all four legs.

Lemurs aren't capable of making complex facial expressions like humans and other primates can, so they rely on other forms of communication such as scent marking and calls.

...

Lemurs are a female-dominant society! In every group of lemurs (within species that form groups) there is a female leader.

The females will often fight the males for food or kick them out of their territory.

Although all lemurs live on Madagascar (and the nearby Comoro Islands), each species has a preference for habitat.

For example, **Sibree's dwarf lemurs** live in the high-altitude rainforests, while **white-collared lemurs** live in the moist, lowland forests.

• • •

Ring-tailed lemurs are the only primates that sleep in the same cave every night.

THEIR FUTURE

THE FUTURE ISN'T BRIGHT FOR LEMURS, BUT WE CAN ALL HELP CHANGE THAT.

Sadly, lemurs are considered to be the most endangered mammal in the world. Around 90% of lemur species are threatened with extinction.

...

The biggest threat to lemurs is **habitat loss**. However, illegal pet trading, bushmeat hunting, and climate change all contribute to the decline in lemur populations.

Coquerel's sifaka lemur.

A young ring-tailed lemur.

Many people want to keep lemurs as pets, but they rarely survive when they are not in a zoo under expert supervision or in the wild. Some species, such as sifaka lemurs rarely survive even under experts' care.

...

Since humans arrived on Madagascar, all species of lemur over 22 lb (10 kg) have become extinct.

...

Surprisingly, most Malagasy people do not even know what 'endangered' means, or that lemurs only exist on Madagascar.

There are many conservation groups, in Madagascar and around the world, that are working to protect lemurs, such as the *World Wide Fund for Nature, Madagascar Fauna Group*, and *Lemur Conservation Network.*

• • •

World Lemur Day is celebrated on the last Friday of October each year. There are lots of events held worldwide, and online, to help raise awareness of lemur conservation efforts. It is a great opportunity to raise money and share information on your social media networks.

A red ruffed lemur.

There are lots of ways you can help lemurs wherever you are in the world. You can make a donation to one of the many lemur conservation foundations, sponsor a lemur, or take part in volunteer work. Even sharing information on social media is helping out!

...

Rosewood is illegally logged in Madagascar and plays a devastating role in destroying lemurs' homes. If you see rosewood items for sale, do not buy them.

Did you know that you can help lemurs simply by changing your search engine? Ecosia.org donates 80% of its profits from searches to plant trees in areas such as Madagascar.

OTHER FUN LEMUR FACTS

FROM THE WILD TO THE WONDERFUL.

Lemurs have wet noses, like dogs.

• • •

The **blue-eyed black lemur** (family: *lemuridae*) is the only primate, other than humans, to have blue eyes.

• • •

Dwarf lemurs store fat in their tails so that they have enough nourishment for the dry season.

A blue-eyed black lemur, which aren't always black! *Photo: Clément Bardot*

Lemurs have two tongues! As well as their primary tongue, lemurs have a secondary tongue called the **sublingua**, which is used to remove hair and dirt from their toothcomb. A **toothcomb** is the upper front set of teeth that is used for grooming.

Lemurs play an important role in maintaining forest biodiversity as they are **seed dispersers**. As they forage around the forest, seeds get stuck in their fur and they fall out in new places. Many plants wouldn't exist anymore if it weren't for lemurs!

...

Ruffed lemurs are considered to be the world's most prolific pollinators. Pollen from plants gets stuck on their noses as they sniff around for food.

Lemurs know how to use the forest's resources as their own personal pharmacy. For example, **red-fronted brown lemurs** will eat millipedes as a cure for parasites, such as worms.

...

Lemurs communicate in different ways. **Indri lemurs**, for example, sing beautifully in a capella together, while others just use the scent of their urine to get their message across!

...

Lemurs are the world's oldest primates. They first evolved over 70 million years ago, long before humans.

The name 'lemur' comes from the Latin word *'lemures'* that refers to the wandering spirits in ancient Roman mythology.

• • •

A group of lemurs is called a **troop**.

• • •

Fossils show that early lemurs had a grooming, or toilet claw.

< **A black and white ruffed lemur.**

In Madagascar, lemurs play an important role in the local culture. *Fady* are cultural taboos or stories that are passed down from generation-to-generation and provide the do's and don'ts for life.

An example of one features the indri lemur, which the locals believe contains the spirits of their ancestors — therefore you should never harm an indri lemur. The aye-aye lemur, on the other hand, is believed to be evil and that if you see one in the wild bad things will happen to you.

Sadly, this has meant that many aye-aye lemurs are killed by locals.

Lemurs have become an important part of popular culture in the past few years. Many films including *Madagascar*, *Dinosaurs* and the documentary *Lemur Street* have leading characters played by fictional or real lemurs.

• • •

All species of lemur except the ring-tailed lemur) have a special reflective layer in their eye called the **tapetum lucidum**. This layer helps to improve night vision and makes their eyes look shiny.

LEMUR *QUIZ*

Now test your knowledge in our Lemur Quiz! Answers are on page 89.

1 How many families of lemurs are there?

2 There used to be lemurs the size of gorillas. True or false?

3 Which sense is most important to lemurs?

4 What is the population of Madagascar?

5 Which family of lemurs do mouse and dwarf lemurs belong to?

6 Are ring-tailed lemurs herbivores or omnivores?

Ring-tailed lemurs.

THE ULTIMATE LEMUR BOOK

7   What is a ring-tailed lemur's favorite food?

8   Are sportive lemurs nocturnal or diurnal?

9   How do sifaka lemurs get around when on the ground?

10   Aye-aye lemurs have a special way of searching for food. What is it called?

11   What are baby lemurs called?

12   When do young lemurs start eating solid food?

13   What does bamboo contain that is poisonous to most animals?

14 Which species of lemurs hibernate?

15 What do you call a group of lemurs?

16 Is a male or female the boss of a group of lemurs?

17 Which species of lemur often sleeps in a cave at night?

18 What percentage of lemurs are threatened by extinction?

19 What is the biggest threat to lemurs?

20 Lemurs have two tongues. What is the second tongue called?

ANSWERS

1. Eight.
2. True.
3. The sense of smell.
4. 27 million.
5. Cheirogaleidae.
6. Herbivores.
7. Tamarind leaves.
8. Nocturnal.
9. They hop forward, which looks like they're dancing.
10. Percussive foraging.
11. Pups.
12. At around two months.
13. Cyanide. However, bamboo lemurs can eat it safely.
14. Mouse and dwarf lemurs.
15. A troop.
16. Female.
17. Ring-tailed lemur.
18. Around 90%.
19. Habitat loss.
20. The sublingua.

Lemur
WORD SEARCH

```
F D S I F A K A P Y D A
G E W O O L L Y E R E B
T R N J F S E C X Z N Z
R H I W E R F M V B D X
E G A N B G F D U S A D
M A D A G A S C A R N E
M Y G E T T Q H Z T G T
J E H F R N A G F R E J
K A T P E J S I N D R I
G Y R G U Q W E L B E N
D E S D F P N H G E D B
S F G R E S S N H G D S
```

A red-bellied lemur.

Can you find all the words below in the word search puzzle on the left?

LEMUR	RING-TAILED	AYE-AYE
MADAGASCAR	SIFAKA	PUPS
ENDANGERED	INDRI	WOOLLY

THE ULTIMATE LEMUR BOOK

SOLUTION

		S	I	F	A	K	A			
		W	O	O	L	L	Y		E	
	R				E				N	
		I				M			D	
			N				U		A	
M	A	D	A	G	A	S	C	A	R	
	Y				T				G	
	E				A				E	
	A		P			I	N	D	R	I
	Y			U			L		E	
	E				P			E	D	
					S				D	

SOURCES

"The IUCN Red List of Threatened Species." 2026. IUCN Red List of Threatened Species. Accessed January 20. https://www.iucnredlist.org/.

"Animals Populated Madagascar by Rafting There." 2010. ScienceDaily. ScienceDaily. https://www.sciencedaily.com/releases/2010/01/100120131159.htm.

Lemur Conservation Network. 2025. "Top 10 Facts About Lemurs." Lemur Conservation Network. October 28. https://www.lemurconservationnetwork.org/top-10-facts-about-lemurs/.

Lemurs. 2026. Accessed January 20. https://www.britannica.com/animal/lemur-primate-suborder.

"Aye-Aye - Wikipedia". 2021. *En.Wikipedia.Org*. https://en.wikipedia.org/wiki/Aye-aye.

"List Of Lemur Species - Wikipedia". 2021. *En.Wikipedia.Org*. https://en.wikipedia.org/wiki/List_of_lemur_species.

"Facts About Lemurs". 2021. *Livescience.Com*. https://www.livescience.com/55276-lemurs.

"Sublingua - Wikipedia". 2021. *En.Wikipedia.Org.* https://en.wikipedia.org/wiki/Sublingua

Oliver Smith. 2021. " 17 Amazing Facts About Madagascar, The Island It Took Humans 300,000 Years To Discover". *The Telegraph.* https://www.telegraph.co.uk/travel/destinations/africa/madagascar/articles/facts-about-madagascar/.

Kautz, Emily. 2019. "Fifteen Fascinating Facts About Lemurs". *Good Nature Travel.* https://www.nathab.com/blog/fifteen-facts-lemurs/.

Platt, John. 2014. "Crisis In Madagascar: 90 Percent Of Lemur Species Are Threatened With Extinction". *Scientific American Blog Network.* https://blogs.scientificamerican.com/extinction-countdown/crisis-in-madagascar-90-percent-of-lemur-species-are-threatened-with-extinction/.

"How To Help – Lemur Conservation Network". 2021. *Lemur Conservation Network.* https://www.lemurconservationnetwork.org/how-to-help/.

We hope you learned some awesome facts about lemurs! We'd love it if you left us a **review**—it always makes us smile :) And more importantly, reviews help other readers make better buying decisions.

Visit us at
www.bellanovabooks.com
for the latest books, blog posts and giveaways!

ALSO BY JENNY KELLETT

... and more!

Available at

www.bellanovabooks.com

and all major online bookstores.

www.ingramcontent.com/pod-product-compliance
Lightning Source LLC
LaVergne TN
LVHW050133080526
838202LV00061B/6480